TEN LITTLE MONKEYS

illustration **danny brooks dalby**

color & design **shannon osborne thompson**

Dalmatian Press ®

ISBN: 1-40371-630-7
© 2001 Dalmatian Press, LLC. All rights reserved.
Printed in the U.S.A.

The DALMATIAN PRESS name and logo are trademarks of
Dalmatian Press, LLC, Franklin, Tennessee 37067.

11269 Ten Little Monkeys
05 06 07 NGS 10 9 8 7 6 5 4 3 2 1

In a jungle
	far away,
Tiny monkeys
	run and play.

1 one

Through banyan branches,
just for fun,
Hunt for monkeys.
You'll find *one.*

High up, playing
peek-a-boo
Around a palm tree,
you'll find *two.*

two
2

three **3**

Swinging on vines
from tree to tree,
Find them and count,
one, two, *three.*

4 four

See the monkeys
more and more.
Playing leapfrog,
you'll find *four.*

5

five

Splashing in
a fern-brimmed brook,
You'll find *five*
if you just look.

six

6

They have fun
with stones and sticks.
If you hunt,
you will find *six.*

Picking flowers
and eating fruit,
There are *seven* —
Aren't they cute?

Near tall trees
and grassy huts,
eight play ball
with coconuts.

8
eight

Standing, waving
in a line,
And somersaulting,
you'll find *nine.*

9
nine

10 ten

In the trees
and on the ground,
ten monkey friends
can be found.

10

You found monkeys
hidden within,
And learned to count
from *one* to *ten*.